P9-BZT-699

·T· · ·Mobile·®

THE UN-CARRIER

#SlowCookerSunday
Leadership, Life and Slow Cooking with CEO and Chef, John Legere

© 2018. T-Mobile USA, Inc. All rights reserved.

ISBN: 978-1-59849-257-6

Library of Congress Control Number: 2018963241

Creative Director: Patty Raz
Editors: Gina Cohen and Janice Kapner
Art Director: Eric Winters
Lead Designer: Dan Hoffman
Designers: Tom Freisem and Kyle Klube
Project Managers: Samuel Bazemore and Ashley Sytsma
Creative Specialist: Ana Reynolds

Photography by Jonathan T. Bishop and Kristian Marson
Some images used under license from Shutterstock.com

Printed and bound in the United States of America
First printing November 2018

Published by Peanut Butter Publishing
943 NE Boat St.
Seattle, WA 98105
info@peanutbutterpublishing.com

Visit www.t-mobile.com

#SlowCookerSunday

Leadership, Life and Slow Cooking
with CEO and Chef, John Legere

Dedicated to my daughters. To Chrissy, my most helpful videographer—thank you for yelling "IN!" with such undying enthusiasm! And to Lizzy, my top (sous) chef— cooking wouldn't be nearly as much fun without you!

ACKNOWLEDGEMENTS

I would like to thank the millions of T-Mobile customers, future customers, and even the trolls who tune in every Sunday on Facebook Live to watch me put ingredients into a slow cooker, chat about all things T-Mobile and—most importantly—who don't judge me when my cake comes out lopsided. I've said all along...the reason I slow cook is because even when you screw it up...it still tastes good!

I'd also like to thank my *Slow Cooker Sunday* crew. The camera operators, sous chefs, hype-people and PAM-shufflers. *Slow Cooker Sunday* wouldn't be possible without the help of my daughters Chrissy and Lizzy, Dave Carey and Patty Raz and her talented team—without whom, my videos would still be sideways.

Let's cook!

Contents

®

Foreword by **Martha Stewart**

Now, I want you to know that I have been a CEO, a full-time chef, an entrepreneur, an Emmy-winning television personality and an expert at slow cooking (my book *Martha Stewart's Slow Cooker* was published in 2017). I am feeling a bit competitive with John Legere since he has followed a similar path and has just written this book, *#SlowCookerSunday*. I have gone through this book with a fine-tooth comb and must admit that it's pretty good!

I like it because it's more than just a book full of great recipes for cooking. It's also a primer for all of us who want some great advice on how to be a great CEO and a successful entrepreneur. John is known in the business world as an unconventional leader, and reading his bold quotes in the book belies that unconventionality and reveals a sensible, straight thinker who gets to the nitty gritty of business problems, listens and acts instead of vacillating and asks questions to get to the bottom of a challenging conundrum.

All the while, by the way, cooking up a storm of delicious and creative and well-acknowledged recipes, demonstrating them on TV while wearing

a magenta leisure suit in a black and magenta and silver monogrammed outfit with a black toque clearly marked CEO, never letting us forget that T-Mobile and slow cooking have gone hand in hand on his road to amazing success!

We are also reminded that John takes chances. For heaven's sake, he hired Snoop Dogg and me to star in a Super Bowl commercial for T-Mobile. We had so much fun re-living our partnership on our TV show, *Martha and Snoop's Potluck Dinner Party*, making references, of course, to Snoop's use of forbidden substances in his cooking, so lots of greens and cans of bisque while hugging purple cushions! I know Snoop, who just published his first cookbook, will use this book just as often as I will—because not only do we love John Legere and his business acumen, but also his "bon mots" about business!

Thanks, John! Maybe now that you have a book to promote, you'll come on the next season of *Potluck Dinner Party*???

Martha Stewart

THE MAN ...IN!... THE MAGENTA CHEF'S HAT
I love my slow cooker.

A few years ago, as a single dad and a CEO with a crazy-busy life, struggling to stay healthy and active, I re-discovered the power of the slow cooker. Easy meals. Healthy meals (most of the time). Meals that made the house smell so good and brought back memories, reminding me of my Irish mother and childhood days growing up...more on that later. And, I loved having meals waiting for me after a long day of doing battle with the competition. Perfect!

So, I cooked in it. A lot.

When I get into something, I really dig in. I found myself searching online for new recipes—even experimenting with some of my own—making tons of great (and some not-so-great) food, talking about it at work and even sharing some of my meals there. As I rode my Segway around the office, plotting our next moves against AT&T and Verizon, people began to ask, "What's going into the slow cooker next?" Slow-cooking began to catch on around the office...and I knew I had to go bigger.

If you know anything about me, you know I'm a pretty huge fan of social media, and I spend hours every day just listening and talking to customers and potential customers from all over. You have to be where your customers are, and you have to be authentic, so in addition to exchanges about T-Mobile, I started sharing pictures of my slow cooker creations, just to see what people thought (and trust me...my meals were not all very pretty!)...

...and people seemed to get a kick out of it. Food is something that seemingly everybody has an opinion on and likes to talk about.

At first, no one believed that I was really cooking for myself this way. The CEO of T-Mobile *slow-cooking?* But as people began oohing (and sometimes booing) over pics of my creations, asking for my recipes by the dozens—then by the hundreds—and began sharing their own, I realized I was tapping into something.

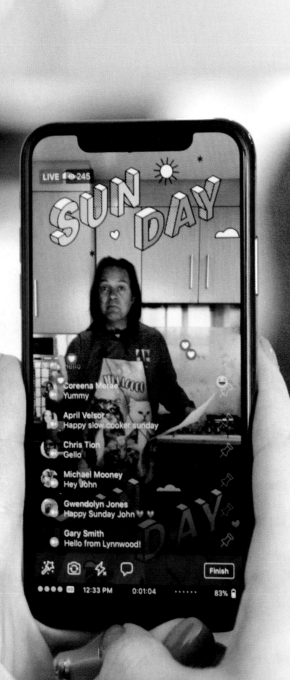

NOT QUITE A
FOOD NETWORK STAR

Around that time, Facebook invited me to try out Facebook Live. I was a heavy Periscope user—usually running around various cities (literally), visiting with customers and employees, sharing what I eventually called "RunScopes"—so I figured why not do the same with my meals? I was already slow-cooking every Sunday anyway. Might as well enjoy a little banter while I was at it!

My first show didn't go well at all. I had my tripod, my phone and my slow cooker. I tapped "Go Live" and put the phone on my tripod. Standing in my kitchen, I talked through the recipe. (One of my own, made with mushrooms, onions, brussels sprouts, chicken thighs and two different types of red sauce. Delicious...to me at least!) I made some jokes and showed off my "skills."

Still streaming live, I pulled my phone off the tripod to check for comments or questions. I was excited to see the steady stream of comments, "likes" and inevitable compliments about my culinary skills. Most comments were, "You're sideways!" "My neck hurts, but this is fun" and "John! You're crooked!" I'd locked my phone in "portrait" mode! Yep, true story!

So, for my big live debut, I was sideways. I tried to play it cool and thanked everyone for watching. I was about to delete it, convinced it was unsalvageable, when a friend called—she was laughing (*at* me, not *with* me, or so she says) and encouraged me to leave it. "It's real," she said, "CEOs—they're just like us!" Still unconvinced, I texted a couple other people and ultimately decided to leave it up—in all its neck-wrenching glory! Not every hit show has a great pilot!

Then I tried again...and the second time around, I got it right. (My third episode was sideways again. But that was the only other time...so far.) Lesson learned!

THE RISE OF SLOW COOKER SUNDAY

Roughly 16,000 people watched that first *Slow Cooker Sunday* in February 2016 (*sorry* for all the sore necks and chiropractic visits!). That was about 15,999 more than I'd expected (I'd asked my friend Dave Carey to tune in). I was stunned. And I had zero idea what to expect next.

As more people tuned in week to week, I got some help filming, so I could focus on cooking and talking with viewers. I did a show every Sunday, no matter where I was—even hotel rooms and airports. Today, a couple years in and 150 episodes later, more than *5 million people* watch each week. I still make mistakes—just like Emeril or Bobby Flay. While I'm not a real cook, and can't even imagine cooking at their level, they keep it real...and I *always* keep it real—which is exactly what I love about *Slow Cooker Sunday*!

And everyone's invited! I've had celebs like Martha Stewart, Snoop Dogg and Kate Hudson join me on the show. World-renowned Din Tai Fung even invited me to film my two-year anniversary episode as the first amateur cook welcomed behind the glass! That was absolutely amazing! But the best part of *Slow Cooker Sunday* is interacting with all the people who tune in. I can't count the number of times I've been out somewhere and heard somebody say, "Hey, it's the guy with the cooking show!" It doesn't matter that I'm covered in magenta and T-Mobile logos. I'm not the CEO. I'm The Slow Cooker Guy. I love that.

This book features 52 of my very favorite slow cooker recipes—other people's recipes that I've adapted and enjoyed—one for every Sunday of the year. I have organized them around a story, around a theme, around my approach to work *and* cooking. That's right—of course it's an "Un-usual" way to approach a cookbook...would you expect anything else from the Un-CEO? I have always been a little irreverent so take my advice: have fun! Break some rules, you never know what you might just cook up! And if you feel like making Christmas Ham for Halloween, do it—call it Hamoween, make it your own. If it tastes right, it can't be wrong.

Every recipe can be made with a basic slow cooker and the kitchen tools you've got lying around. And, in each chapter, I share some of my secrets to success that translate directly from business to the kitchen. If you've been watching me cook for a while, you know what I always say...the ingredients hit my slow cooker, and I say..."IN!" So each tip can be applied IN the office and IN the kitchen.

So, dive in, enjoy...and don't forget to share your pics and thoughts with me on social @JohnLegere or Facebook.com/JohnJLegere.

See you on the next *Slow Cooker Sunday*!

CHAPTER ONE

STAND FOR SOMETHING & DON'T BE A CHICKEN

STAND FOR SOMETHING
IN THE OFFICE

Becoming CEO of T-Mobile was always about more than a job. From the start, it was about taking on a cause. I knew what we would stand for. I knew too well that carriers had been treating customers terribly for too long. The Un-carrier was going to disrupt the wireless industry and unleash the single most-important technology of our lifetime—in a totally new way. Customers loved their smartphone, but HATED their carrier! We were going to change wireless for the good of consumers.

We crafted a manifesto that gave voice to our cause—a rallying cry and clear statement of who we were and what we stood for. We united around that cause.

The passion and potential I saw in our people was unleashed. They had a purpose, a goal and a common enemy—the carriers! When that happened, we became unstoppable.

So, whether you're tasked with running a business or managing a project, think about your cause, your why. Write it down. Declare it. Reflect on it. Become unstoppable.

STAND FOR SOMETHING
IN THE KITCHEN

I'm gonna get literal with "stand for something" here. First, a little backstory.

So, I told you I was a runner. All these years, running's always been a part of my life. So many good memories. Like the summer I ran the Olympic torch relay for the 1984 Summer Games. I was on a team sponsored by Saucony. Three or four times a day, we'd get dropped out of a bus, run a five-minute mile, holding that torch up, with a big, billowing flame on top. Insane. But awesome. I still have that uniform somewhere (I don't think it fits anymore, though).

I still run. I still like to keep moving. And one thing I love about cooking is that it gives me a chance to keep moving while I'm at home. And *Slow Cooker Sunday* has given me a way to share what I love and get other people up and moving. If you've watched even one episode, you'll know I like to do a little something I call the PAM Shuffle. It's kind of my signature thing. I spray PAM on the floor, shuffle around on it, do a dance. For real. You're not doing it right if you're not winded afterwards. And it's catching on. It's working! People post, tweet and share videos of themselves doing it all the time!

So even if you're not all that into slow-cooking, that's okay. It's still a great way to get moving and get a few extra steps in. Go ahead, spray a little PAM on the floor. Shuffle a little. Got kids? Give them something to laugh at. And get them in on the fun! Show them it's a blast to be active, cook it slow, make a meal—and make some memories.

DON'T BE A CHICKEN!

DELICIOUS DISHES THAT AREN'T CHICKEN

In business, and in the kitchen, you gotta be willing to take some risks, to go against the grain, to be bold. Be willing to make mistakes and learn from 'em—it'll make you a better person and a better chef!

To inspire you, start with one of these non-chicken delicious dishes...

TARRAGON LAMB SHANKS WITH CANNELLINI BEANS

FILIPINO BEEF AFRITADA

CORNED BEEF AND CABBAGE

SPAGHETTI SQUASH AND MEATBALLS

GREAT CHILI MEATLOAF

BEER BRATS

MELT-IN-YOUR-MOUTH POT ROAST

FRENCH BEEF BURGUNDY

SCALLOPED POTATOES AND HAM

VEGETARIAN LENTIL SLOPPY JOES

APPLE DUMP CAKE

BEER-BRAISED SHORT RIBS

POLENTA

CHRISTMAS HAM

Tarragon Lamb Shanks with Cannellini Beans

Recipe Adapted From: asweetandsavorylife.com

Aired on Facebook LIVE: 12/18/2016

Slow Cooker Size: 7 or more quarts
Serves 12 people

Ingredients

- 4 (1.5-pound) lamb shanks
- 1 (19-ounce) can cannellini beans or other white beans, rinsed and drained
- 1½ cups carrot, diced and peeled
- 1 cup onion, chopped
- ¾ cup celery, chopped
- 2 cloves garlic, thinly sliced
- 2 teaspoons dried tarragon
- ½ teaspoon salt
- ¼ teaspoon freshly ground black pepper
- 1 (28-ounce) can diced tomatoes, undrained

Steps

- Trim fat from lamb shanks. Place beans and next 4 ingredients (through garlic) in the slow cooker; stir well. Place lamb shanks on bean mixture; sprinkle with tarragon, salt and pepper. Pour tomatoes over lamb. Cover and cook on high for 1 hour. Reduce heat to low and cook for 9 hours or until lamb is very tender.

- Remove lamb shanks from the slow cooker. Pour bean mixture through a colander or sieve over a bowl, reserving liquid. Let liquid stand 5 minutes; skim fat from the surface of the liquid. Return bean mixture to liquid. Remove lamb from bones; discard bones. Serve lamb with bean mixture.

Filipino Beef Afritada

Recipe Adapted From: theskinnypot.com

Slow Cooker Size: 4 to 7 quarts
Serves 6–8 people

Ingredients

- 1 pound boneless beef for stew, cut into bite-sized pieces
- 5-inch long carrots, cut into small cubes
- 2 medium-sized potatoes, cut into small cubes
- 1 (8-ounce) can tomato sauce
- ½ large red bell pepper, cut into small cubes
- 1 cup frozen green peas
- 1 (14.5-ounce) can low-fat and low-sodium chicken or beef broth
- 4 pieces small hot dogs (little smokies)
- 1 teaspoon brown sugar, to taste and salt

Steps

- Put the beef in the bottom of the slow cooker.
- Add in potatoes, carrots, bell pepper and hot dogs.
- Pour in the chicken or beef broth and set the slow cooker on high for 4 hours and 6 hours on low.
- When ready, add in the tomato sauce and mix. Continue cooking for 10 to 15 minutes and add frozen green peas. Turn off the slow cooker. Let it sit for few more minutes and serve.

Aired on Facebook LIVE:
2/26/2017

Corned Beef and Cabbage

Recipe Adapted From: foodiecrush.com

Aired on Facebook LIVE: 3/12/2017

Slow Cooker Size: 5 to 7 quarts
Serves 6–8 people

Ingredients

- 3 carrots, peeled and cut into 3-inch pieces
- 1 yellow onion, peeled and quartered
- ½ pound small potatoes, halved
- 1 corned beef brisket (about 3 pounds) plus pickling spice packet or 1 tablespoon pickling spice
- 1⅓ (12-ounce) beers
- 6 sprigs fresh thyme
- ½ head Savoy cabbage cut into 1½-inch wedges
- ½ cup sour cream
- 3-4 tablespoons prepared horseradish, to taste

Steps

- Place the carrots, onion and potatoes into the slow cooker.
- Place corned beef, fat side up, on top of the vegetables and sprinkle with pickling spice.
- Pour the beers over the vegetables and brisket.
- Sprinkle with the sprigs of fresh thyme. Cover and cook on high until corned beef is tender, 5 to 6 hours on high or 10 to 12 hours on low.
- Arrange cabbage over corned beef, cover and continue cooking until cabbage is tender, 45 minutes to 1 hour or 1½ to 2 hours on low.
- Meanwhile, mix the sour cream and horseradish together. Thinly slice the corned beef against the grain and serve with the vegetables and cooking liquid with the horseradish sauce.

Spaghetti Squash and Meatballs

Recipe Adapted From: alldayidreamaboutfood.com

Slow Cooker Size: 6 to 7 quarts
Serves 4 people

Ingredients

- 1 medium spaghetti squash
- 1½ cups crushed tomatoes
- ½ teaspoon salt
- ½ teaspoon garlic powder
- ¼ teaspoon pepper
- ¼ teaspoon dried oregano
- 16 meatballs
- 2 tablespoons butter or olive oil
- Additional salt and pepper, to taste

Steps

- Cut spaghetti squash in half, crosswise. Place in the bottom of the slow cooker, cut-side down.
- In a processor or blender, combine tomatoes, salt, garlic powder, pepper and oregano. Puree until smooth. Pour into the bottom of the slow cooker.
- Place meatballs over tomatoes, around spaghetti squash. Cook on low for 6 to 7 hours or on high for 3 to 4 hours.
- Using tongs and kitchen gloves, remove spaghetti squash from the slow cooker. Scoop out seeds and discard. Scoop out flesh into a sieve or colander and let drain a few minutes to reduce moisture. Transfer to a bowl and toss with butter or olive oil.
- Divide between 4 plates and top with sauce and meatballs.

Aired on Facebook LIVE:
10/15/2017

"OUR MISSION IS CHANGING WIRELESS FOR GOOD —ALL OF WIRELESS."

Great Chili Meatloaf

Recipe Adapted From: recipe4living.com

Aired on Facebook LIVE: 2/19/2017

Slow Cooker Size: 4 to 7 quarts
Serves 6–8 people

Ingredients

- 2 pounds ground turkey or lean ground beef
- 1 cup onion, chopped
- ⅔ cup Italian-style seasoned breadcrumbs
- ½ cup green bell pepper, chopped
- ½ cup chili sauce
- 4 cloves garlic, minced
- 2 eggs, slightly beaten
- 2 tablespoons Dijon mustard
- 1 teaspoon salt
- ½ teaspoon Italian seasoning
- ¼ teaspoon black pepper
- Salsa (for topping)

Steps

- In a large bowl, mix all ingredients except salsa. Shape into a round loaf and place on foil strips (see tip below) in the slow cooker. Cover and cook on low for about 5 to 6 hours, or until juices run clear. Remove from slow cooker and top with salsa, if desired.

Tip: Tear off 3 or 4 pieces of aluminum foil about 12-18 inches long (depending on size of slow cooker). Fold to 3 or 4-inch width and place crisscrossing in the slow cooker. These will make it easier to lift out the meatloaf.

Beer Brats

Recipe Adapted From: themagicalslowcooker.com

Aired on Facebook LIVE: 4/9/2017

Slow Cooker Size: 5 or more quarts
Serves 12 people

Ingredients

- 2 (14-ounce) packages smoked bratwursts
- Cooking oil
- 1 large white onion, sliced
- 2 bell peppers, sliced
- 1 to 2 cloves garlic, minced
- ½ teaspoon pepper
- 1 (12-ounce) can beer
- Mustard (optional)
- Buns for serving

Steps

- In a large skillet over medium-high heat, add enough cooking oil to cover the bottom. Add the brats and brown them on all sides; this can be done in 2 batches.
- While the brats are browning, add the onion, bell peppers, garlic and black pepper to the slow cooker.
- Add the browned brats on top of the onion and peppers. Pour over the beer.
- Cover and cook on high for 3 hours.
- Serve the brats, onions and bell peppers over rolls. Top with mustard if desired.

Melt-In-Your-Mouth Pot Roast

Recipe Adapted From: joyouslydomestic.com

Aired on Facebook LIVE: 10/16/2016

Slow Cooker Size: 4 to 7 quarts
Serves 4–6 people

Ingredients

- 1 chuck roast (about 3 pounds)
- Olive oil
- 1 pound carrots, peeled and cut into large chunks
- 2 pounds potatoes, peeled and cut into large chunks
- 1 onion, peeled and cut into large chunks
- 2 stalks celery, cut into large chunks (optional)
- 1 cup beef broth
- 1 tablespoon corn starch

For the seasoning mix:

- 2 tablespoons steak seasoning
- 1 tablespoon kosher salt
- 1 tablespoon dried thyme
- 1 tablespoon dried rosemary

Steps

- Combine together seasoning mix in a small bowl. Set aside.
- Coat both sides of meat with olive oil. Sprinkle on a third of the seasoning mix onto each side.
- Sear both sides of the meat in a large skillet over medium-high heat. Transfer roast to the slow cooker.
- Place the vegetables in a large bowl. Drizzle on a little olive oil to coat the vegetables. Sprinkle on the remaining seasoning mix. Add the vegetables to the same skillet that was used to sear the meat. Sauté for about 5 minutes, stirring occasionally.
- Transfer the vegetables to the top of the roast in the slow cooker. Pour in the beef broth. Cover with lid.
- Cook on low for 9 hours or on high for 6 hours.
- Using a turkey baster, retrieve most of the cooking juices from the slow cooker. Transfer juices to a small sauce pan and bring to a simmer over medium heat on the stovetop. Whisk together the cornstarch with a little water. Blend in the pan juices while whisking. Bring back to a simmer until thickened. Taste and adjust seasoning as needed.
- Transfer the roast and vegetables to a large platter. Ladle the gravy over. Serve immediately.

French Beef Burgundy

Recipe Adapted From: geniuskitchen.com

Aired on Facebook LIVE: 12/31/2017

Slow Cooker Size: 4 to 7 quarts
Serves 4 people

Ingredients

- ¼ cup flour
- ½ teaspoon salt
- ½ teaspoon pepper
- 2 pounds boneless beef chuck, cut into 1-inch cubes
- 2 tablespoons olive oil
- 1 onion, sliced
- 8 button mushrooms, sliced
- ½ cup fresh parsley, minced
- 3 cloves garlic, minced
- 2 bay leaves
- 1 cup Burgundy wine
- ½ cup beef broth

Steps

- Combine the flour, salt and black pepper.
- Dredge the beef cubes in the flour mixture and brown in the olive oil in a medium skillet.
- Place the beef and remaining ingredients into the slow cooker and mix thoroughly.
- Cover; cook on low for 4 to 6 hours or on high for 2 to 3 hours.

I WAS A PRETTY BAD KID

I come from a big Irish Catholic family. As the middle of five children growing up outside Boston, I was no angel. I still remember sitting in class, the teacher would ask a question, and I'd find a way to turn the answer into a joke or to give some unconventional—but correct—response. I guess I'm still that kid. Too much restless energy. Bored with the status quo. Looking for a fresh take.

I burned off a lot of that energy running. I was good...and I knew it. So, my mom, a strong Irish woman, took on the duty of keeping me humble. She'd tell me, "John, you're not as good as you think you are. You're no better than your brothers and sisters." It was tough love, but I needed it!

After high school, I wanted to be an Olympian. My dad had different ideas for me. He had very humble upbringings—whatever money he had was in his pocket. I was talking to Harvard...oh man, he wanted me to go to there so badly. But the suit and tie and starched, button-down shirt he dreamed of for his boy sounded like a straight-jacket to me. My dream job? Running. Then maybe coaching. To Dad's credit, he supported me. He let that Harvard dream go. And it's no matter—I never would have gotten in, anyway. 😉

Instead I went to the University of Massachusetts—where all the top runners were at that time—and majored in physical education. I ran. I was living the dream. Then, one day, I sat down to take a test. One question involved drawing up a budget to live on a gym teacher's salary. And I couldn't spin the answer.

That wasn't exactly the life I'd dreamed of. As I tried to imagine other futures, I thought about where I'd come from. I thought about that smart-ass kid in the classroom—a restless rule-breaker. What kind of career made sense for a guy like that? Obviously, I went a pretty different route...

Paul, Mary, Mom and me at Whalom Park

All the Legere kids in front of our home

1984 Olympic Torch Relay

Early 80s running for Saucony in Massachusetts

The early days with my siblings

Scalloped Potatoes and Ham

Recipe Adapted From: allrecipes.com

Slow Cooker Size: 4 to 7 quarts
Serves 8 people

Ingredients

- 5 pounds red potatoes, peeled and sliced
- ¾ cup chopped onion
- ¼ teaspoon black pepper
- ½ teaspoon salt
- ¼ cup (½ stick) butter, cut into pats
- 4 cups cubed ham
- ½ cup water
- 1 pint whipping cream

Steps

Layer in this order:

- Sliced potatoes on the bottom.
- Spread onions on top of potatoes.
- Sprinkle with salt and pepper.
- Add whipping cream evenly.
- Place butter pats evenly on top.
- Layer with cubed ham.
- Pour water over top.
- Cover and cook on high for 5 hours or until potatoes are tender. After about 4 hours, stir and recover for the last hour.

Aired on Facebook LIVE:
5/14/2017

Vegetarian Lentil Sloppy Joes

Recipe Adapted From: simplyquinoa.com

Aired on Facebook LIVE: 5/28/2017

Slow Cooker Size: 4 to 7 quarts
Serves 6 people

Ingredients

- 1 cup carrots, finely chopped
- 1 cup mushrooms, finely chopped
- 1 cup onions, finely chopped
- 2 garlic cloves, minced
- 1½ cups brown lentils
- ½ cup quinoa
- 1 (8-ounce) can tomato sauce
- ½ cup ketchup
- 2 tablespoons maple syrup
- 2 tablespoons hot sauce
- 2 tablespoons mustard
- 1 tablespoon chili powder
- 1 teaspoon paprika
- Pinch of salt and pepper
- 3 to 4 cups vegetable broth

Steps

- Add everything into the slow cooker, starting with 3 cups of broth. Stir to combine, cover and set to high. Cook on high for 2 to 3 hours (or on low for 4 to 6). Check and add more liquid as needed.
- Serve warm with a bun, biscuit or over spaghetti squash!

Apple Dump Cake

Recipe Adapted From: crazyforcrust.com

Slow Cooker Size: 4 to 7 quarts
Serves 8–10 people

Ingredients

- 5 to 7 Granny Smith apples
- ¼ cup granulated sugar
- 1½ teaspoons cinnamon divided
- 1 box yellow cake mix
- ½ cup oats, quick cook or old-fashioned
- 1 stick (½ cup) butter, sliced

Steps

- Peel, core and slice the apples. Use up to 7 if the apples are small but use closer to 5 if they're large. Apples should be thin and bite sized.
- Spray slow cooker with PAM.
- Place apples in the bottom of the slow cooker. Sprinkle with sugar and ½ teaspoon of cinnamon.
- Place the cake mix in a large bowl. Add the oats and 1 teaspoon of cinnamon. Stir, then sprinkle over the top of the apples.
- Drop slices of the butter over the top of the cake mix.
- Cover and cook on high for 4 hours. Start checking at 1½ hours. Once all the butter is melted, the powder is gone and the top is golden, it is done. Remove it after about 2 hours so the condensation helps to dissolve the cake mix. Serve with ice cream or whipped cream.

Aired on Facebook LIVE:
4/15/2017

Beer-Braised Short Ribs

Recipe Adapted From: itsyummi.com

"Don't be dissuaded by the beer here—if you're not a fan, don't worry—you won't taste it. It just makes for an incredibly flavorful dish you're gonna make more than once."

Slow Cooker Size: 5 to 7 quarts
Serves 4–6 people

Ingredients

- 3 medium onions cut into wedges
- 3 pounds bone-in beef short ribs trimmed of fat
- 1 bay leaf
- 1 (12-ounce) can light beer or non-alcoholic beer
- 2 tablespoons brown sugar
- 2 tablespoons Dijon mustard
- 2 tablespoons tomato paste
- 2 teaspoons dried thyme
- 2 teaspoons beef bouillon granules
- 1 teaspoon salt
- ¼ teaspoon pepper
- 3 tablespoons all-purpose flour
- ½ cup cold water

Steps

- Place onions in the slow cooker; add ribs and bay leaf. Combine the beer, brown sugar, mustard, tomato paste, thyme, bouillon, salt and pepper. Pour over meat. Cover and cook on low for 8 to 10 hours or until meat is tender.

- Remove meat and vegetables to a serving platter; keep warm. Discard bay leaf. Skim fat from cooking juices; transfer juices to a small saucepan. Bring liquid to a boil. Combine flour and water until smooth. Gradually stir into the pan. Bring to a boil; cook and stir for 2 minutes or until thickened.

Polenta

Recipe Adapted From: inthekitchenwithkath.com

"The great thing about polenta is that it makes a perfect base for so many other slow-cooked meals. Try it underneath some chili!"

Slow Cooker Size: 4 to 7 quarts
Serves 8–10 people

Ingredients

- PAM
- 7½ cups water
- 1½ cups polenta
- 1½ teaspoons of salt
- 2 cups freshly grated Parmesan cheese
- 2 tablespoons butter
- Additional salt and pepper, to taste

Steps

- Spray the inside of the slow cooker with PAM.
- Add the water to the slow cooker. Whisk in the polenta and salt.
- Cover and cook on low for 4 to 6 hours.
- Stir in the Parmesan cheese and butter.
- Season to taste with salt and pepper.
- Serve immediately or hold on warm for 1 to 2 hours. If held on warm, stir in a bit of hot water if it thickens up too much.

Christmas Ham

Recipe Adapted From: allroadsleadtothe.kitchen

Aired on Facebook LIVE: 12/24/2017

Slow Cooker Size: 4 to 7 quarts
Serves 6–8 people

Ingredients

- 2 small onions, peeled and halved
- 10 black peppercorns
- 2 whole-star anise
- 2 bay leaves
- big pinch of ground cloves
- 1 (6 to 7 pound) smoked pork picnic shoulder (ham)
- 2 cups water
- 1 cup apple cider

For the glaze:

- ¼ cup lingonberry jam
- 2 tablespoons honey
- ½ teaspoon ground allspice
- ⅛ teaspoon ground cloves

Steps

- Place the onion halves in the bottom of a the slow cooker, cut-side down. Scatter peppercorns, star anise, bay leaves and ground cloves around them. Using them as a stand, set the pork shoulder on top of the onions, skin side facing up. Pour the apple cider and water over the pork. Cover and cook on low for 6 to 8 hours or on high for 4 hours until the ham registers at least 160°F in the center.
- When the ham is done, preheat oven to 425°F.
- Thoroughly line a 9-inch by 13-inch baking dish with heavy-duty foil or a couple of layers of regular foil. Carefully lift the ham out of the slow cooker and set it carefully into the pan.
- Use a sharp knife and some tongs to remove the skin and all but a thin layer of fat. Use a knife to score the fat (diamonds, squares, lines, etc.).
- Stir all of the glaze ingredients together until well combined, then spread the glaze over the scored fat and slide into preheated oven for 25 minutes.
- Remove ham from the oven and let rest for at least 15 minutes before slicing.

"I made this while wearing a magenta Santa outfit. I had the hardest time sourcing the right ham. First, they delivered the wrong pork shoulder. Then, they delivered a 25-pound ham, and it didn't come close to fitting in my slow cooker! I had to trek to Whole Foods to get the right one."

CHAPTER TWO

SHUT UP AND LISTEN & SPICE THINGS UP

SHUT UP AND LISTEN!
IN THE OFFICE

I get a lot of requests to speak with business school students, and I love talking with the leaders of tomorrow. It's energizing. And, when the questions invariably arise about the keys to successful business leadership, I tell them I can distill everything they need to know into a few words. Then I wait for their hands to hover over their keyboards, and I say, "Listen to your employees, listen to your customers, shut the f%!# up and do what they tell you."

Some type it into their notes. Some look at me like I'm nuts.

It's so insanely simple. But it's true. You would not believe how many leaders—and companies—get this wrong. The higher we rise, the more deference we're given, the more we forget how to shut up and listen.

When I'm in one of our stores I ask three questions, "How's business? Are you making any money? How can I help?" Then I just listen. The answers to these questions tell me almost everything I need to know to run T-Mobile.

The same goes for our customers. I spend so much time listening on social because it's such a powerful and real way to connect. As CEO, people tend to tell you what you want to hear. Not so on Twitter! As harsh as the feedback may be at times, it's incredibly valuable and it gives me an edge.

It's really that simple. Shut up and listen—never stop learning from everyone around you.

WHAT'S NEXT?

"My philosophy is…listen to employees and listen to your customers, shut the F up and do what they tell you!

#SlowCookerSunday: Leadership, Life and Slow Cooking with CEO and Chef, John Legere

SHUT UP AND LISTEN!

IN THE KITCHEN

I can cook it slow with the best of them. But I am under no illusion that I'm a great chef. Far from it. So I listen and learn from the incredible creativity and talent of seasoned pros. I take in everything I can from my fellow vloggers and bloggers. I build from their recipes and I make them my own.

The point is, you've got to be open to the conversation. The fact that you picked up this book says you get that. Maybe you know I've spent the past 150-plus Sundays with my slow cooker. You know I've put in the time and work to make sure you're getting only the best I've got. So, you're already applying Success Secret #1.

SPICE THINGS UP

SPICY MEALS

I love to poke fun at Big Red and the DeATThstar. I call 'em out at every opportunity, and I'm not afraid to get in there, to throw a little spice into the mix the way other CEOs wouldn't dare. In the kitchen, get a little adventurous. You'll be surprised how adding a bunch of flavor can rock your whole world.

Start with these spicy meals...

POLLO GUISADO

CHILI-SOY CHICKEN WITH BOK CHOY

CHIPOTLE-LIME CHICKEN THIGHS WITH JAMAICAN RICE

RED LENTIL CURRY

SPICY BEEF TORTELLINI SOUP

HONEY-BUFFALO DRUMSTICKS

BUFFALO CHICKEN SLIDERS

SLOW-AS-YOU-GO PULLED CHICKEN

BRAZILIAN CHICKEN CURRY

JAMBALAYA

GINGER CHICKEN CONGEE

CHICKEN CURRY

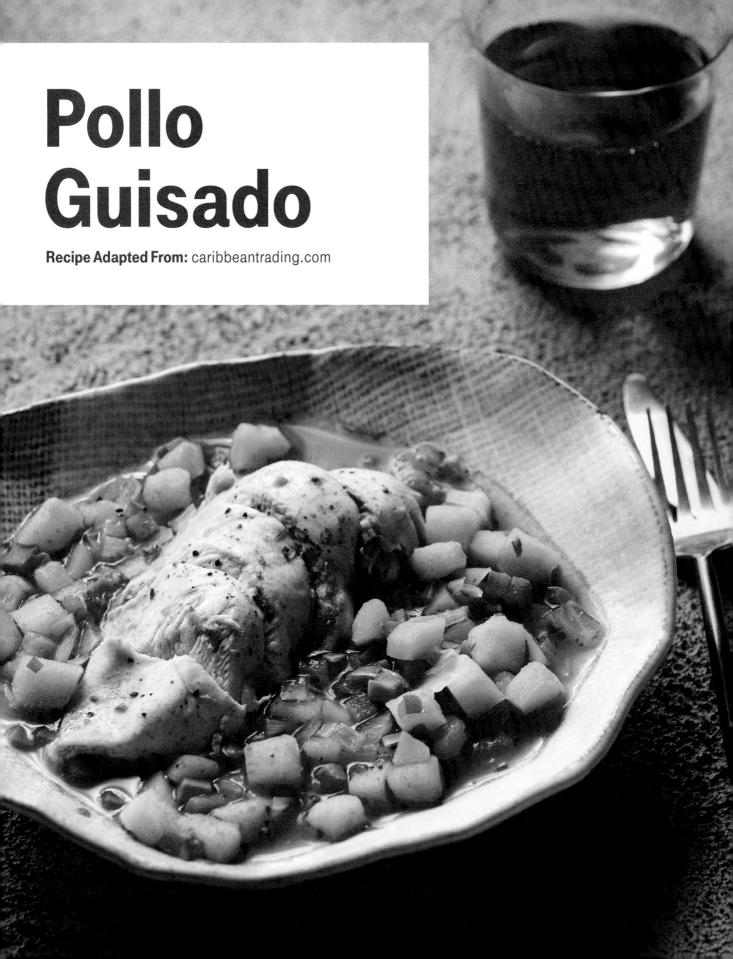

Pollo Guisado

Recipe Adapted From: caribbeantrading.com

Slow Cooker Size: 4 to 7 quarts
Serves 4–6 people

Ingredients

- 16-ounce boneless, skinless chicken breast or tenderloins
- 3 potatoes (about 1 cup)
- 3 carrots, peeled and cut
- 2 tablespoons of sofrito
  (a jarred Spanish seasoning sauce, look for it in the ethnic foods aisle)
- 2 tablespoons of tomato sauce
- 2 packets of sazón
- ½ cup onions, chopped
- ½ cup green bell peppers, chopped
- 2 cups chicken broth

Steps

- Add all ingredients into the slow cooker and cook on low for 6 to 8 hours.

Aired on Facebook LIVE:
3/19/2017

"When I picked up my phone off the tripod to respond to questions and comments, it kept flipping sideways on me! Whoops!"

Chili-Soy Chicken with Bok Choy

Recipe Adapted From: countryliving.com

Aired on Facebook LIVE: 4/2/2017

Slow Cooker Size: 5 to 7 quarts
Serves 4 people

Ingredients

- 3 tablespoons low-sodium soy sauce
- ½ cup low-sodium chicken broth or water
- 3 tablespoons brown sugar
- 2 tablespoons fresh lime juice
- 1 tablespoon fresh ginger, grated
- 2 teaspoons chili garlic sauce
- 2 cloves garlic, minced
- 2½ pounds boneless, skinless chicken thighs
- 2 teaspoons cornstarch
- 1 cup long-grain white rice
- 4 heads baby bok choy
- Scallions, sliced
- Sesame seeds, toasted

Steps

- In the slow cooker, whisk together the chicken broth, soy sauce, sugar, lime juice, ginger and chili garlic sauce; stir in the garlic.
- Add the chicken to the slow cooker and cook, covered, until the chicken is cooked through and easily pulls apart, 4 to 5 hours on high or 6 to 7 hours on low.
- Twenty-five minutes before serving, if the slow cooker is on low, increase to high. In a small bowl, whisk together the cornstarch and 2 tablespoons of the cooking liquid, then stir the mixture into the slow cooker and cook, covered, for 20 minutes.
- Meanwhile, cook the rice according to package directions. Eight minutes before serving, using two forks, break the chicken into smaller pieces. Separate the bok choy leaves, then gently fold them into the chicken mixture and cook, covered, until heated through, 2 to 4 minutes. Serve with the rice and sprinkle with scallions and sesame seeds if desired.

"My daughter Chrissy and I both wore T-Mobile ONEsies during this episode. They were made as an April Fool's joke, but we pretended they were really a 'thing' throughout this entire show. We had a good laugh."

Chipotle-Lime Chicken Thighs with Jamaican Rice

Recipe Adapted From: robinmillercooks.com

Aired on Facebook LIVE: 9/25/2016

Slow Cooker Size: 4 to 7 quarts
Serves 4 people

Ingredients

Chipotle-Lime Chicken Thighs:

- 1 cup onion, sliced
- 1 cup celery, chopped
- 1 cup carrots, chopped
- 4 pounds skinless chicken thighs
- Salt and freshly ground black pepper
- 1 (15-ounce) can tomato sauce
- ¼ cup lime juice
- 1 tablespoon chipotle chilis, minced, in adobo sauce with 1 teaspoon sauce from can
- 2 cloves garlic, minced
- 1 avocado, diced
- ¼ cup fresh cilantro leaves, chopped
- Lime wedges, for garnish

Jamaican Rice and Peas:

- 2 cups instant white rice
- 1 (14-ounce) can coconut milk
- 1 cup water
- 1 (15-ounce) can red beans, drained
- 1 teaspoon dried thyme
- ½ teaspoon finely grated lime zest
- ¼ cup scallions, chopped
- Salt and freshly ground black pepper

Steps

For the chicken:

- Arrange onion, celery and carrots in the bottom of the slow cooker. Season chicken thighs with salt and pepper and arrange over vegetables.

- In a medium bowl, whisk together tomato sauce, lime juice, chipotle chilis with sauce and garlic. Pour mixture over chicken.

- Cover and cook on low for 6 to 8 hours or on high for 3 to 4 hours. Serve half of the thighs with this meal (topped with diced avocado and cilantro and garnished with lime wedges) and reserve remaining thighs for another meal.

For the rice:

- In a medium saucepan, combine rice, coconut milk, water, beans, thyme and lime zest. Set pan over high heat and bring to a simmer. Reduce heat to low, cover and simmer for 5 minutes until liquid is absorbed. Fold in scallions and season, to taste, with salt and pepper.

Red Lentil Curry

Recipe Adapted From: pinchofyum.com

Aired on Facebook LIVE: 9/3/2017

Slow Cooker Size: 4 to 7 quarts
Serves 16 people

Ingredients

- 4 cups regular brown or masoor lentils
- 2 onions, diced
- 4 cloves garlic, minced
- 1 tablespoon ginger, minced
- 4 tablespoons butter (optional)
- 5 tablespoons red curry paste
- 1 tablespoon garam masala
- 1½ teaspoons turmeric
- 2 teaspoon sugar
- A few good shakes of cayenne pepper
- 2 (29-ounce) cans tomato puree
- 1 teaspoon salt, to taste
- ½ cup coconut milk or cream
- Cilantro for garnishing
- Rice for serving

Steps

- Rinse the lentils and place them in the slow cooker. Add the diced onions, garlic, ginger, butter, curry paste, garam masala, turmeric, sugar and cayenne. Stir to combine.

- Pour just 1 can of tomato puree over the lentils. Refill the can with water twice and add to the slow cooker. Stir to make sure that the lentils are covered with liquid. Cover and cook on high for 4 to 5 hours or on low for 7 to 8 hours.

- Check once or twice during cooking to add more water or tomato puree if the lentils are soaking up all the liquid. The amount of water or tomato puree you add depends on how soupy you want your lentils to be. Generally,
1½ cans of tomato puree plus the two cans of water is perfect. Taste and season with salt. Lentils will be soft when they are done cooking.

- Stir in the coconut milk and sprinkle with cilantro just before serving. Serve over rice or naan bread.

"There are 'rules' as to what a CEO is supposed to be... stupid rules! And just being who I am...it's working out."

Spicy Beef Tortellini Soup

Recipe Adapted From: slowcookergourmet.net

Slow Cooker Size: 4 to 7 quarts
Serves 6 people

Ingredients

- 1 pound beef-stew meat
- 2 cups spicy marinara or spaghetti sauce
- 3 cups vegetable broth
- 2 (14.5-ounce) cans fire-roasted diced tomatoes (or regularly diced tomatoes if preferred)
- 1 teaspoon Italian seasoning
- 8 ounces dried tortellini pasta noodles
- 2 tablespoons heavy cream (optional)
- Grated Parmesan cheese for serving (optional)

Steps

- Add stew meat, spaghetti sauce, broth, diced tomatoes and Italian seasoning to the slow cooker.
- Cover and cook on low for 7 to 9 hours.
- Remove lid and stir (break up any larger chunks of stew meat if desired).
- Add tortellini pasta and turn slow cooker on high and let cook for 20 to 30 minutes or until the pasta is tender.
- To cut the acidity a bit, stir in 1 to 2 tablespoons of cream; this is optional but does help the flavors work together.
- Serve garnished with grated Parmesan cheese or as desired.

Aired on Facebook LIVE:
9/24/2017

Honey-Buffalo Drumsticks

Recipe Adapted From: thechunkychef.com

Aired on Facebook LIVE: 9/17/2017

Slow Cooker Size: 6 to 7 quarts
Serves 4–6 people

Ingredients

- 4 pounds fresh chicken drumsticks, patted dry

For the rub:

- 2 tablespoons brown sugar
- 1½ teaspoons kosher salt
- 1 teaspoon black pepper
- 1½ teaspoon garlic powder
- 1½ teaspoon onion powder
- 1 teaspoon smoked paprika
- 1 teaspoon chili powder
- 1 teaspoon ground cumin
- 1 teaspoon dried parsley

For the sauce:

- ¾ cup hot sauce
- ½ cup honey
- 1 tablespoon melted butter
- 1 tablespoon molasses

Steps

- In a small mixing bowl, add rub ingredients and stir to combine thoroughly. Spray slow cooker with PAM and add drumsticks. Sprinkle rub over the top and use hands to massage the rub into all the chicken.

- In the empty rub mixing bowl, add sauce ingredients and whisk to combine well. Pour over spiced wings and toss gently to coat. Cover slow cooker and cook on high for 2 hours, or low for 3 to 4 hours.

For the glaze:

- Line a baking sheet with aluminum foil. Place an oven safe cooling wire on it with the cooked drumsticks on top. Pour sauce from the slow cooker into a saucepan. Add 2 tablespoons cornstarch and 2 tablespoons of water to a small bowl and whisk, then pour into sauce and whisk. Cook over medium-high heat until boiling. Reduce heat to medium-low and whisk as it cooks. Cook about 5 minutes, or until thickened to desired consistency.

- Brush drumsticks with sauce, then broil on high for 2 to 3 minutes. Brush with more glaze and broil another 2 minutes. You should now have perfectly sticky wings!

#SlowCookerSunday: Leadership, Life and Slow Cooking with CEO and Chef, John Legere

Buffalo Chicken Sliders

Recipe Adapted From: allfreeslowcookerrecipes.com

Slow Cooker Size: 4 to 7 quarts
Serves 12 sliders

Ingredients

- 4 boneless, skinless chicken breasts
- 1 (12-ounce) bottle buffalo chicken wing sauce
- 2 cups celery, very thinly sliced
- ½ cup thinly sliced red onion
- ⅓ cup ranch dressing
- 1 package 12 dinner rolls

Steps

- Spray slow cooker insert with PAM. Sprinkle chicken with salt and pepper. Reserve 2 tablespoons of the buffalo wing sauce. Pour the rest over the chicken in the slow cooker and cook on low for 3 to 4 hours.
- Remove chicken and sauce from the cooker. Place chicken on a cutting board and shred with two forks and place into a medium bowl.
- Spoon some of the cooking sauce over the chicken and toss well. Return to the cooker to keep warm.
- In a small bowl, toss the celery with the onion and ranch dressing and add the reserved buffalo wing sauce.
- Warm the rolls. Assemble and serve the sliders with some of the celery slaw spooned onto each one.

Aired on Facebook LIVE:
7/2/2017

UDE,
OU GOTTA
O BACK
O WORK

After bailing on my dreams of being a gym teacher, I switched majors and got a degree in accounting. My plan was to go to a Big Eight accounting firm. But fate called. I took a job with New England Telephone, then AT&T, where I did a deep dive learning the ins and outs of the telecom industry.

After too many years of that, I needed to change it up. At the time, Michael Dell was pulling together a group of people for his leadership team. Any one of them could've been a CEO, but we all jumped at the chance to be part of this A-Team. An amazing experience. I wouldn't have traded it for anything. After that, I became CEO of Asia Global Crossing, then Asia Global *and* Global Crossing, and then Global Crossing. That was trial by fire.

Then, in the span of a few weeks, I left my job and my marriage ended. Boom. Suddenly, for the first time in a long time, I had time on my hands. Too much time. Time to take a look at the man in the mirror. And I saw a guy I barely knew, in his mid-50s, who'd spent way too much of his life in a suit— that wasn't the life I'd wanted for myself when I was young.

But I had no idea what would come next. I read Eckhart Tolle's *The Power of Now*. Eye-opening. I took my daughter's

Various executive positions at major companies that required suits...never again!

advice and got on Match.com. Cringing. I re-arranged my house. And I was running...and running and running. Miles and miles a day.

And, for the first time in my life, I learned to dread the question, "What do you do?" I hated that question. What do I do? How does a 50-something man say, "I don't know yet?" After a few months of this, my friends told me straight up, "Dude, you gotta go back to work." But

what could I do without losing sight of the guy I'd just begun to recognize in the mirror?

I had been recruited for a new job I was considering, but right on cue, an old friend—a headhunter—reached out to ask a favor. Would I meet with some people about a job as CEO of T-Mobile? At the time, things weren't looking good for them. As a business, reports were that they were barely hanging on. But, I was *Power of Now*'ing.

We met. And I listened. And, the more I heard, the more it seemed to me that there was something incredibly good about this company. I saw people who wanted to do something better for their customers—something totally revolutionary in wireless. I saw heart. I saw huge potential and I wanted in.

Slow-As-You-Go Pulled Chicken

Recipe Adapted From: sweetbabyrays.com

Aired on Facebook LIVE: 9/17/2017

Slow Cooker Size: 4 to 7 quarts
Serves 4–5 people

Ingredients

- 2 cups yellow onions, thinly sliced
- 2 tablespoons garlic, chopped
- 3 cups reduced-sodium chicken stock
- 1 tablespoon kosher salt
- 1 tablespoon coarse ground black pepper
- 2 teaspoons ground cumin
- 4 to 5 pounds chicken breast
- 1 (10-ounce) bottle of your favorite Sweet Baby Ray's Barbecue Sauce (I like Sweet 'n Spicy, myself)

Steps

- Place the onions and garlic in an even layer in the slow cooker and pour in the stock. Season chicken breast with salt, pepper and cumin. Place the meat on top of the onions and garlic.
- Cover with your favorite barbecue sauce and cook until the chicken is fork tender, approximately 3 to 4 hours on high or 6 to 7 hours on low.
- Remove the chicken and place on a cutting board. Using 2 forks, shred the chicken into pieces.
- Serve with your favorite sauce.

Brazilian Chicken Curry

Recipe Adapted From: geniuskitchen.com

Aired on Facebook LIVE: 8/21/2016

Slow Cooker Size: 4 to 7 quarts
Serves 6–8 people

Ingredients

- 1½ to 2 pounds chicken breasts or chicken thighs, skinless (bones okay if you want them in there for the flavor)
- ¾ cup coconut milk
- 1 cup chicken broth
- 2 tablespoons tomato paste
- 3 cloves garlic, minced
- 1 tablespoon ground ginger
- 4 to 6 tablespoons curry powder (increase or decrease, to taste)
- 2 bell peppers, chopped into cubes (any color)
- 1 yellow onion, thinly sliced
- Salt and pepper, to taste
- 1 dash red pepper flakes

Steps

- Cut chicken pieces in half or quarters (not cubed, just cut up enough to make it all fit in the slow cooker).
- Combine coconut milk, tomato paste, garlic, ginger, curry powder, salt and pepper and red pepper flakes in the slow cooker and whisk together.
- Add in peppers, chicken and broth.
- Mix all ingredients together to completely cover the chicken in the curry mixture.
- Cover and cook on low for 6 to 8 hours or on high for 4 to 5 hours.

Jambalaya

Recipe Adapted From: allrecipes.com

Slow Cooker Size: 4 to 7 quarts
Serves 12 people

Ingredients

- 1 pound boneless, skinless chicken breast halves, cut into 1-inch cubes
- 1 pound andouille sausage, sliced
- 1 (28-ounce) can diced tomatoes with juice
- 1 large onion, chopped
- 1 large green bell pepper, chopped
- 1 cup chopped celery
- 1 cup chicken broth
- 2 teaspoons dried oregano
- 2 teaspoons dried parsley
- 2 teaspoons Cajun seasoning
- 1 teaspoon cayenne pepper
- ½ teaspoon dried thyme
- 1 pound frozen cooked shrimp without tails

Steps

- In the slow cooker, mix the chicken, sausage, tomatoes with juice, onion, green bell pepper, celery and broth. Season with oregano, parsley, Cajun seasoning, cayenne pepper and thyme.
- Cover, and cook 7 to 8 hours on low or 3 to 4 hours on high. Stir in the shrimp during the last 30 minutes of cook time.

Aired on Facebook LIVE: 3/5/2017

"Would you believe I filmed this episode in a Las Vegas hotel? It was great. We celebrated Mardi Gras together—one of my most memorable episodes!"

Ginger Chicken Congee

Recipe Adapted From: epicurious.com

"Alright, it's a fancy name but a simple recipe—a congee is just an Asian rice porridge. They often eat it for breakfast in China."

Slow Cooker Size: 4 to 7 quarts
Serves 8 people

Ingredients

- 2 pounds boneless, skinless chicken thighs
- 8 cups chicken stock
- 1 cup long-grain rice
- 3 small dried red chiles, such as Thai or chile de arbol
- 1 (3-inch) piece ginger, thinly sliced
- 2 garlic cloves, pressed
- 1½ teaspoons kosher salt

For serving:
Cubed avocado, lime wedges, cilantro, sliced jalapeño, sliced scallions, chopped peanuts, chili oil, fish sauce, hot sauce, soy sauce, and/or crispy fried shallots (choose as many as you like)

Steps

- Place chicken, stock, rice, chilis, ginger, garlic and salt into the slow cooker. Cover and cook on low for 8 hours.
- Remove chilis and ginger. Stir, breaking up chicken into bite-size pieces. Divide congee among bowls. Serve with an assortment of toppings alongside.

Chicken Curry

Recipe Adapted From: thelemonbowl.com

Slow Cooker Size: 4 to 7 quarts
Serves 2–3 people

Ingredients

- 1 pound boneless, skinless chicken breasts
- 1 medium onion, thinly sliced
- 15 ounces chickpeas, drained and rinsed
- 2 medium sweet potatoes, peeled and diced
- ½ cup coconut milk
- ½ cup chicken stock, low sodium
- 15 ounces tomato sauce
- 2 tablespoons curry powder, salt-free
- 1 teaspoon salt
- ½ teaspoon cayenne powder (optional)
- 1 cup green peas, frozen
- 2 tablespoons lemon juice
- Cilantro (optional garnish)

Steps

- In the bottom of the slow cooker, whisk together coconut milk, chicken stock, tomato sauce, curry powder, salt and cayenne.
- Add chicken breasts, onion, chickpeas and sweet potatoes. Using tongs, gently toss ingredients together to ensure they're evenly coated.
- Cook on low for 8 hours or on high for 4 hours.
- Stir in peas and lemon juice 5 minutes before serving.
- Serve over rice and with plenty of fresh cilantro.

"Go as spicy as you like on this one—add a little more cayenne if that's your thing."

CHAPTER THREE

SHAKE UP THE STATUS QUO & SPOON UP SOMETHING NEW

SHAKE UP THE STATUS QUO
IN THE OFFICE

Only a few years ago, anybody with a phone could've told you that carriers had made a mess of wireless. Coming in as the new CEO at T-Mobile, I remember telling a roomful of reporters, "If you came down from Mars and saw the way wireless was run, you'd get back in your spaceship and go back to where you came from." A lot of wireless customers would've been happy to join them.

In case you've mentally blocked those days out—I can't blame you!— here's a refresher...

Remember confusing charts of daytime, nighttime and weekend minutes, message and data limits? Remember cutting conversations short so you wouldn't burn through your minutes? Remember coming home to bill-shock when you forgot to turn off your phone before that trip to Canada? Remember the pages of taxes and fees added to your bill? Remember surprise data overage charges?

Becoming the Un-carrier meant becoming the opposite of all of that—and dragging the rest of the industry kicking and screaming along with us. We wanted to do more than fix wireless for our own customers. We wanted to change wireless for everyone on the planet. We wanted to disrupt the status quo and change wireless for good. So we've spent the past 6 years doing just that!

Of course, disrupting the status quo meant taking some big risks for the sake of doing what was right for customers. As those risks began to pay off, as the wireless revolution took hold, something pretty cool began to happen. I saw more and more people—employees and customers— wearing their magenta with new pride. Our competitors ripped off their uniform the second their shift was over. If T-Mobile employees changed their clothes after work, it was only to put on MORE magenta!

It spread like crazy. I began seeing more magenta in and outside of work, in selfies on social media, and the requests began pouring in from customers for magenta shirts, jackets, shoes, hats—yep—even chef's hats!

We were all part of something bigger. And that rebel spirit was contagious.

SHAKE UP THE STATUS QUO
IN THE KITCHEN

When it comes to cooking, shaking up the status quo can mean a whole lot of things.

Sometimes it means re-thinking typical meals. What would a new spin on that bacon and egg breakfast look like? Want yogurt and granola for dinner? Who's stopping you? We tend to eat within the confines of what we consider breakfast, lunch and dinner, but who says we even need that? You like to graze all day? Feel like putting all you've got into one big, beautiful pot roast? Do what works for you. Break some rules!

And, of course, that goes for the ingredients you use, too. You've been leaning on the same basic casserole for years. Could it be better? How will you know unless you get out of that comfortable rut and do a little experimenting? Throw in some spinach and mushrooms. Try it with zucchini noodles if you're into that kind of thing. When was the last time you experimented with a little fusion in your slow cooker? Vietnamese paella, anyone? Cooking should be fun. So, as long as you're enjoying yourself and trying new things, you're good.

Put your own spin on these recipes and see how things turn out. And, hey, if you don't love the results, bring it into work. I guarantee the food will get eaten!

SPOON UP SOMETHING NEW

In life, and in the kitchen, you've gotta change things up every once in a while, and you've gotta surprise people—and yourself! Got a great idea for a way to do things differently? Don't keep it to yourself. And when you're cooking, be willing to try something new. You never know what you may end up loving.

And while you're at it, spoon up some of these incredible soups, stews and chilis...

PUMPKIN CHICKEN CORN CHOWDER

VEGETARIAN LENTIL TORTILLA SOUP

SPLIT PEA SOUP

LENTIL AND QUINOA CHILI

ROOT VEGETABLE STEW

CREAMY CHICKEN AND WILD RICE SOUP

CHICKEN TORTELLINI SOUP

CHILI WITH BLACK BEANS AND CORN

MAINE CORN CHOWDER

THAI CHICKEN SOUP

TURKEY CHILI

TOMATO BASIL CHICKEN STEW

Pumpkin Chicken Corn Chowder

Recipe Adapted From: pressurecookingtoday.com

"With Halloween right around the corner when I filmed this, I wore a fake 'bloody' chef's hat and apron and held a fake butcher knife—really got into the spirit!"

Slow Cooker Size: 4 to 7 quarts
Serves 6 people

Ingredients

- 2 tablespoons butter
- 1 cup onion, diced
- 1 garlic clove, minced
- 2 (14.5-ounce) cans chicken broth
- 1 (15-ounce) can pumpkin puree
- ½ teaspoon Italian seasoning
- ¼ teaspoon freshly ground black pepper

- ⅛ teaspoon dried red pepper flakes
- ⅛ teaspoon freshly grated nutmeg
- 2 large russet potatoes, cubed
- 2 large boneless, skinless chicken breasts, uncooked and diced
- 2 cups frozen corn
- ½ cup half and half

- Salt and additional ground pepper, to taste
- Bacon, crumbled (optional)
- Cilantro leaves, torn (optional)

Steps

- In a medium skillet, heat the butter over medium heat. Add the onions and sauté until the onions are translucent. Add garlic and cook for 1 minute more.
- Add the potatoes and corn to the bottom of the slow cooker, followed by the onions and garlic.
- Add chicken broth, pumpkin puree, Italian seasoning, pepper, red pepper flakes and nutmeg. Stir to combine.

Aired on Facebook LIVE: 10/29/2017

- Cook on high for 4 to 6 hours until the potatoes are soft. Stir in cream. Add salt and pepper, to taste.
- Top with crumbled bacon and cilantro (optional).

Vegetarian Lentil Tortilla Soup

Recipe Adapted From: shugarysweets.com

Aired on Facebook LIVE: 10/22/2017

Slow Cooker Size: 4 to 7 quarts
Serves 6 people

Ingredients

- 1 (15-ounce) can black beans, drained and rinsed
- 1 (15-ounce) can pinto beans, drained and rinsed
- 1 (15-ounce) can sweet corn, drained
- ¾ cup dried lentils
- ¾ cup onion, diced
- 1 green pepper, seeded and diced
- 1 jalapeño pepper, seeded and diced
- 4 cups vegetable broth
- 1 (15-ounce) can tomato sauce
- 2 tablespoons tomato paste
- ¾ cup salsa verde
- 1 teaspoon cumin
- 1 teaspoon chili powder
- 1 teaspoon garlic powder
- 1/4 teaspoon red pepper flakes
- 1 teaspoon kosher salt
- ½ cup heavy whipping cream (optional, and add right before serving)

Toppings:
- Pico de gallo
- Greek yogurt
- Sour cream
- Tortilla strips
- Jalapeños
- Cheddar cheese, shredded
- Avocado or guacamole

Steps

- Add black beans, pinto beans, corn, lentils, onion, green pepper, jalapeño pepper, vegetable broth, tomato sauce, tomato paste, salsa, cumin, chili powder, garlic powder, red pepper flakes and salt to the slow cooker. Stir to combine.

- Cover and cook on low for 6 to 8 hours. If desired, right before serving, add in heavy whipping cream. Stir and serve. Top with your favorite toppings and enjoy!

Split Pea Soup

Recipe Adapted From: tabsandtidbits.com

Aired on Facebook LIVE: 1/1/2017

Slow Cooker Size: 4 to 7 quarts
Serves 4–6 people

Ingredients

- 1 pound (16-ounce package) dried green split peas, rinsed
- 1 large leek (light green and white portion only), chopped and thoroughly cleaned
- 3 celery ribs, diced
- 2 large carrots, diced
- 1 garlic clove, minced
- ¼ cup fresh parsley, chopped
- 6 cups vegetable broth
- ½ teaspoon ground black pepper
- 1 teaspoon salt, to taste
- 1 bay leaf

Steps

- Pour all of the ingredients into the slow cooker and stir to combine. Cover and cook on low for 7 to 8 hours or on high for 3 to 4 hours. Remove and discard bay leaf before serving.

Lentil and Quinoa Chili

Recipe Adapted From: aggieskitchen.com

"A perfect vegetarian/vegan meal you can throw together with stuff that's probably already in your pantry and fridge."

Slow Cooker Size: 4-7 quarts
Serves 6–8 people

Ingredients

- 1 onion, chopped
- 3 garlic cloves, minced
- 1 celery stalk, chopped
- 2 bell peppers, chopped
- 1 (15-ounce) can diced tomatoes
- 4 cups vegetable broth
- 1 can water
- 1 cup dried lentils
- 1 (15-ounce) can pinto beans
- 2 tablespoons chili powder
- 2 teaspoons cumin
- 1 tablespoon oregano
- ½ cup uncooked quinoa

Steps

- Place all ingredients into the slow cooker. Cook on low heat for 8 hours.
- Serve chili with your favorite fixings: shredded cheese, plain Greek yogurt or sour cream, avocado, green onion and cilantro.

Root Vegetable Stew

Recipe Adapted From: chowhound.com

Slow Cooker Size: 4 to 7 quarts
Serves 2–3 people

Ingredients

- ¼ cup olive oil
- 2 medium yellow onions, large dice
- Kosher salt
- 1¼ teaspoons ground ginger
- 1 (3-inch) cinnamon stick
- ½ teaspoon ground coriander
- ¼ teaspoon ground cumin
- ⅛ teaspoon cayenne pepper
- Pinch saffron threads
- Freshly ground black pepper
- 1 pound Yukon Gold potatoes (about 3 large), large dice
- 1 pound carrots (about 4 to 5 medium), peeled and large dice
- 1 pound parsnips (about 4 medium), peeled and large dice
- 3 cups low-sodium chicken or vegetable broth
- 2 pounds sugar baby pumpkin or butternut squash (about 1 small), peeled, seeded and large dice
- 1 pound sweet potatoes (about 2 medium), peeled and large dice
- 1 (15-ounce) can chickpeas, also known as garbanzo beans, drained and rinsed (about 1½ cups)
- ½ cup golden raisins, also known as sultanas
- 1 bunch spinach, trimmed and washed (about 4 cups loosely packed)
- 1½ tablespoons cider vinegar, plus more as needed

Steps

- In the bottom of the slow cooker, whisk together coconut milk, chicken stock, tomato sauce, curry powder, salt and cayenne.
- Add chicken breasts, onion, chickpeas and sweet potatoes. Using tongs, gently toss ingredients together to ensure they're evenly coated.
- Cook on low for 8 hours or on high for 4 hours.
- Stir in peas and lemon juice 5 minutes before serving.
- Serve over rice and with plenty of fresh cilantro.

I OFTEN TELL MY FRONTLINE EMPLOYEES, AS LONG AS I CAN HEAR YOU, AND YOU CAN HEAR ME, WE'RE GOLDEN."

Creamy Chicken and Wild Rice Soup

Recipe Adapted From: topslowcookers.com

Slow Cooker Size: 5 or more quarts
Serves 4–6 people

Ingredients

- 1½ cups uncooked wild and brown rice blend
- 1 package bare, boneless, skinless chicken thighs (about 1½ pounds)
- 1 large onion, diced (a heaping cup)
- 2 cups celery, chopped
- 2 cups carrots, chopped
- 2 bay leaves
- 2 teaspoons dried parsley
- ½ teaspoon dried thyme
- ½ teaspoon ground sage
- ½ teaspoon garlic powder
- ½ teaspoon ground black pepper
- ½ teaspoon salt
- 4 cups no-salt-added chicken stock
- 3 cups water
- ½ cup heavy cream
- Milk or water as necessary to thin soup

Steps

- Combine all ingredients except cream in the slow cooker.
- Cook on low for 6 to 8 hours. Remove bay leaves and discard. Remove chicken thighs and shred and return to slow cooker.
- Place ½ cup of heavy cream into a medium bowl. Slowly whisk 1 to 2 cups of hot soup into cream. Then, slowly pour that mixture back into the slow cooker while whisking.
- Taste and season with salt and pepper as needed before serving.

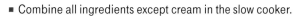

Aired on Facebook LIVE: 4/23/2017

Chicken Tortellini Soup

Recipe Adapted From: therecipecritic.com

Aired on Facebook LIVE: 10/9/2016

Slow Cooker Size: 4 to 7 quarts
Serves 4 people

Ingredients

- 1½ pounds boneless chicken breast
- 3 medium carrots, peeled and diced
- 3 stalks celery, diced
- 1 medium onion, diced
- 3 cloves garlic, minced
- 6 cups low-sodium chicken broth
- 1 cup water
- 2 bay leaves
- 1 teaspoon Italian seasoning, or more to taste
- 2 cups cheese tortellini
- Fresh parsley chopped, if desired
- Salt and pepper, to taste

Steps

- Add all of the ingredients to the slow cooker except for the tortellini and parsley.
- Cook on low for 6 hours.
- Remove the cooked chicken from the slow cooker, shred or cube, and then add back to the slow cooker.
- Add in the tortellini and cook for 15 minutes or until they are cooked all the way through.
- Season with salt and pepper to taste. Discard bay leaves and serve immediately with chopped parsley, if desired.

Chili with Black Beans and Corn

Recipe Adapted From: chewoutloud.com

Slow Cooker Size: 4 to 7 quarts
Serves 10–12 people

Ingredients

- 2 pounds lean ground turkey or beef
- 1 teaspoon garlic powder
- 1 teaspoon kosher salt
- 1 teaspoon freshly ground black pepper
- 1 to 2 tablespoons light olive oil
- 32 ounces tomato sauce
- 1 (16-ounce) can Italian diced tomatoes, with juices
- 2 (16-ounce) cans black beans, drained
- 1 cup frozen sweet corn kernels
- 6 cloves garlic, minced
- 2 green bell peppers, seeded and chopped
- 1 large onion, chopped
- 2 to 4 teaspoons chili powder, depending on desired amount of heat
- 1 teaspoon cumin
- 1 teaspoon salt
- 2 teaspoons sugar
- Dash of cayenne
- Dash of hot sauce
- Dash of allspice

Optional toppings:

- Cheddar cheese, shredded
- Fresh cilantro, chopped
- Fresh lime slices
- Sour cream

Steps

- Mix uncooked ground meat with 1 teaspoon of garlic powder, 1 teaspoon of kosher salt and 1 teaspoon of pepper. Mix together well. Add olive oil in a large skillet and cook meat until browned, breaking it up while you cook.

- Transfer cooked meat to the slow cooker. Add in the rest of ingredients to the browned meat. Cook on low for 6 to 7 hours or on high for 4 to 5 hours.

- Keep warm until ready to serve. Garnish with desired toppings.

Aired on Facebook LIVE:
4/9/2017

Maine Corn Chowder

Recipe Adapted From: themagicalslowcooker.com

Aired on Facebook LIVE: 11/5/2017

Slow Cooker Size: 4 to 7 quarts
Serves 8 people

Ingredients

- 32 ounces chicken broth
- 1 (15-ounce) can cream-style corn
- 1 (15-ounce) can whole kernel corn
- 4 cups Yukon Gold potatoes (about 1 pound), diced
- ½ cup white onion, diced
- 1 red bell pepper, diced
- ¾ teaspoon dried thyme
- ¼ teaspoon black pepper
- 16 ounces bacon, sliced, cooked and drained
- 1 cup heavy cream

Steps

- Add everything except the cream into the slow cooker. Cover and cook on low for 8 hours.
- When the cooking time is done, stir in the cream. Add the salt, to taste, if needed. Serve and enjoy!

BECOMING THE UN-CEO

Although I'd now spent a good portion of my life in a suit, being a "conventional" CEO never felt true to who I am. They wear ties. They sit behind desks and spend their days in the C-suite, where they're insulated and surrounded by people who constantly tell them "yes." Outside the office, they spend their days at country clubs golfing with the same suits, and they rarely—if ever—interact with their customers or employees. So, they never hear what they need to hear. It's BS. And it's just not me.

Being the Un-carrier means being the Un-CEO. I take a completely different approach to management and leadership. I love wide open communication, where every employee knows they're heard. I love frank and unafraid debate and discussion. I'm out there, with employees and customers, completely open and approachable and plugged in. An Un-CEO does all the things a CEO would never do. (Like slow-cooking and live-streaming.)

At T-Mobile, we like to say, "#BeYou." We know we're at our best when we bring our whole selves to work. And I'm incredibly grateful to be surrounded by people who let me be me. I wear my sweats and sneakers to work. (Like a PE teacher!) I ride my Segway up and down the hallways. I've got long hair. That's me.

When I think of where I came from, I think of that smart-ass who went against the grain, the "bad kid" who looked for the twist and the fresh take and did things differently. And I know he'd recognize himself in the mirror all these years later. I hope he'd be proud of who he grew up to be. Magenta chef's hat and all.

Thai Chicken Soup

Recipe Adapted From: foodiecrush.com

Slow Cooker Size: 4 to 7 quarts
Serves 4 people

Ingredients

- 2 tablespoons red curry paste
- 2 (12-ounce) cans coconut milk
- 2 cups chicken stock
- 2 tablespoons fish sauce
- 2 tablespoons brown sugar
- 2 tablespoons peanut butter
- 1½ pounds chicken breasts, cut into 1½-inch pieces
- 1 red bell pepper, seeded and sliced into ¼-inch slices
- 1 onion, thinly sliced
- 1 heaping tablespoon fresh ginger, minced
- 1 cup frozen peas, thawed
- 1 tablespoon lime juice
- Cilantro, for garnish
- Cooked white rice

Steps

- Mix the curry paste, coconut milk, chicken stock, fish sauce, brown sugar and peanut butter in the slow-cooker bowl. Place the chicken breast, red bell pepper, onion and ginger in the slow cooker. Cover and cook on high for 4 hours.
- Add in the peas and cook for ½ hour longer. Stir in lime juice and serve with cilantro and white rice.

Aired on Facebook LIVE:
7/30/17

Turkey Chili

Recipe Adapted From: myrecipes.com

Slow Cooker Size: 5 to 7 quarts
Serves 4 people

Ingredients

- 1¼ pounds lean ground turkey
- 1 large onion, chopped
- 1 garlic clove, minced
- 1½ cups frozen corn kernels
- 1 red bell pepper, chopped
- 1 green bell pepper, chopped
- 1 (28-ounce) can crushed tomatoes
- 1 (15-ounce) can black beans, rinsed and drained
- 1 (8-ounce) can tomato sauce
- 1 (1.25-ounce) package chili seasoning mix
- ½ teaspoon salt

Optional toppings:

- Shredded Colby and Monterey Jack cheese blend
- Red onion, finely chopped

Steps

- Cook the first 3 ingredients in a large skillet over medium-high heat, stirring until turkey crumbles and is no longer pink; drain. Spoon mixture into the slow cooker; stir in corn and next 7 ingredients until well blended.
- Cook on high for 4 to 5 hours or at low for 6 to 8 hours. Serve with desired toppings.

"Talk about a crowd-pleaser. Such an easy recipe that's great for guests—you can sub out the turkey for ground chicken or ground beef, too."

Tomato Basil Chicken Stew

As created by: gimmesomeoven.com

Slow Cooker Size: 4 to 7 quarts
Serves 4–6 people

Ingredients

- 1 tablespoon olive oil
- 1 small white onion, chopped
- 2 carrots, peeled and diced
- 2 stalks celery, diced
- 4 cloves garlic, minced
- 2 (28-ounce) cans whole tomatoes (with their juices)
- 1 (14-ounce) can cannellini beans, rinsed and drained
- 3 cups shredded, cooked chicken
- 2 handfuls baby spinach
- ¼ cup roughly chopped, fresh basil
- 1 teaspoon salt
- ½ teaspoon black pepper
- ¼ teaspoon crushed red pepper flakes

Steps

- Add all ingredients to the slow cooker, stir to combine, cook on high for 3 to 4 hours (or on low for 6 to 8), then serve with freshly grated Parmesan cheese.

CHAPTER FOUR

SHARE
THE
SUCCESS
&
GET
COMFORTABLE
BEING YOU

SHARE THE SUCCESS
IN THE OFFICE

It ought to be clear by now that being the Un-carrier is about more than doing right by our customers. It's also about doing right by our people. You can't have a great company without happy employees who love coming to work, who love what they do, who share a common cause—and an obsession with the customer experience.

So, how do you create, grow and sustain a culture like that? You have everyone share in its success.

For starters, you give every employee—full-time, part-time, store rep and CEO—the same benefits. That's right. At T-Mobile, a part-time Mobile Expert in one of our stores has access to the same awesome benefits as the CTO, COO or CMO. Because, of course they do.

You also take a fresh approach to recognizing great work. At T-Mobile, we have two incredible events every year for top performers across the entire company.

We send them and a plus one on a fully paid vacation somewhere warm and beautiful, and we make damn sure they know how proud we are to have them wearing our colors.

And, this is important. You ensure your employees share in your company's success by making them owners. Literally. T-Mobile is one of only a few companies in America to give EVERY employee stock. People at T-Mobile work like they own this company— because they do.

Success is a hell of a lot more fun when it's shared. And, when you create a culture where people know they're appreciated, they're treated well, they have a sense of ownership and they celebrate one another's successes...you create something truly extraordinary.

IN THE KITCHEN

I've spent a lot of evenings cooking dinner for one. I know how that goes. First, you do the shopping, then spend a bunch of time in the kitchen prepping, chopping, cooking and cleaning. You sit down to eat. Ten minutes later, you're done. Maybe the food tasted amazing. But no one else got to experience your best chili ever. You missed out on the best part of cooking: sharing.

Food is best when shared. When it's paired with good conversation. So, why not call a friend over? Invite a neighbor. Take leftovers and share them at work. Cut loose and start a cooking club! Share your recipes online and get people talking and sharing their own. Widen your circle. Get creative.

And, if you're already sharing meals with family and friends, take it to the next level! Get them into the kitchen with you. Give them something to do. Pawn off the carrot-peeling to the kids. You don't want to do that anyway. And reach out into your community. There's probably a soup kitchen in town that could use your skills or a nearby tent city that would appreciate a hot meal.

And, speaking of sharing, look me up on Facebook or Twitter and share your food pics. You can start with any of these great recipes!

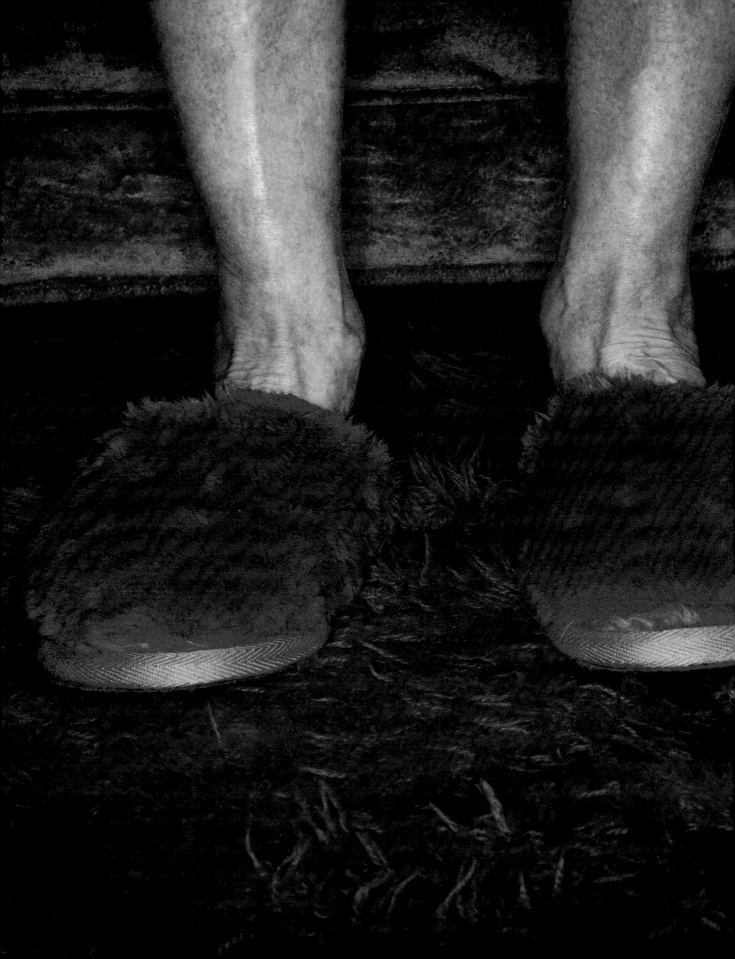

GET COMFORTABLE BEING YOU

COMFORT FOODS

At T-Mobile, we believe that everyone should bring their authentic selves to work every day—and we're better for it. Being yourself will always net the best results. For me, that's my magenta sneakers, my leather jackets and my long hair. So, get comfortable being who you are. And if being who you are in the kitchen means singing as you cook, wearing a funky apron, or yes, even wearing fuzzy slippers—perfect. Tag me in your pics.

These comfort foods are delicious inspiration...

EGGPLANT LASAGNA
STUFFED SHELLS WITH SPINACH
PARMESAN-HERB CHICKEN AND ORZO
VEGGIE OMELET
RAINBOW RISOTTO WITH PEPPERS
BAKED APPLES
CHICKEN CACCIATORE
SLOW-ROASTED CHICKEN WITH VEGETABLES
APPLE PUDDING CAKE
STICKY CHICKEN WINGS
ITALIAN SAUCY CHICKEN THIGHS
CHEESY SPINACH AND MOZZARELLA RIGATONI
CHICKEN TACOS
GIANT CHOCOLATE CHIP COOKIE

Eggplant Lasagna

Recipe Adapted From: sweetcsdesigns.com

#SlowCookerSunday: Leadership, Life and Slow Cooking with CEO and Chef, John Legere

Slow Cooker Size: 4 to 7 or more quarts
Serves 6 people

Ingredients

- 2 eggplants, sliced into long, thin "noodles" (use a mandoline if available)
- 1 onion, diced
- 1 bell pepper, diced
- 1 cup cottage cheese
- 8 ounces shredded mozzarella cheese with 1 ounce reserved for the top
- 12 ounces pasta sauce

Steps

- Layer a few eggplant slices to cover the bottom of the slow cooker.
- Layer a little sauce, peppers, onions, cottage cheese and mozzarella.
- Repeat to make 3 layers with the eggplant, sauce, veggies, cottage cheese and mozzarella.
- Add a final fourth layer of eggplant and top with sauce.
- Cover and cook on high for 2½ hours, or until eggplant is softened.
- Add 1 ounce of reserved cheese to the top, cover.
- Cook for an additional 10 minutes until cheese is melted.
- Garnish with red pepper flakes and parsley if desired.

Aired on Facebook LIVE:
8/6/2017

Stuffed Shells with Spinach

Recipe Adapted From: everydaygoodthinking.com

Aired on Facebook LIVE: 12/11/2016

Slow Cooker Size: 4 to 7 quarts
Serves 8 people

Ingredients

- 1 cup frozen spinach, chopped, thawed and squeezed dry
- 1 (12-ounce) container ricotta cheese
- 3 cups mozzarella cheese, shredded and divided
- ½ cup Parmesan cheese, grated
- 2 cloves garlic, minced
- 1 tablespoon Italian seasoning
- 28 jumbo pasta shells
- 2 (24-ounce) jars marinara sauce
- Parsley, chopped

Steps

- In a large bowl, stir spinach, ricotta cheese, 2 cups of mozzarella cheese, Parmesan, garlic and Italian seasoning.
- Divide and fill each shell with ricotta mixture.
- Add 3 cups of sauce to the bottom of the slow cooker.
- Place 14 stuffed shells in the bottom of the slow cooker. Spoon 2 cups marinara sauce over shells.
- Top with remaining stuffed shells and sauce.
- Cover slow cooker and cook on high for 3 to 4 hours or on low for 6 to 8 until shells are cooked. Remove lid and sprinkle remaining mozzarella cheese over the shells. Wait 5 minutes until the cheese is melted. Garnish with parsley.

Parmesan-Herb Chicken and Orzo

Recipe Adapted From: lecremedelacrumb.com

Aired on Facebook LIVE: 8/27/2017

Slow Cooker Size: 4 to 7 quarts
Serves 6 people

Ingredients

- 4 boneless, skinless chicken breasts or 4 to 6 boneless, skinless chicken thighs
- 3 teaspoons Italian seasoning, divided
- 3 cups low-sodium chicken broth
- 1½ cups orzo pasta
- 4 tablespoons butter, melted
- 1 cup mushrooms, sliced
- 1 medium white or yellow onion, finely chopped
- 2 teaspoons garlic, minced
- 1 teaspoon salt, to taste
- ¼ teaspoon black pepper, or to taste
- ½ cup Parmesan cheese, shaved or finely shredded
- Freshly cracked black pepper and herbs (such as thyme or parsley) for garnish

Steps

- Season chicken with a bit of the Italian seasonings and salt and pepper on both sides. Cook in a large nonstick skillet on the stove over medium-high heat for 1 to 2 minutes on each side until browned on the outsides.
- Transfer chicken to a greased slow cooker. Add chicken broth, butter, mushrooms, onions, garlic and salt and pepper to slow cooker.
- Cover and cook on high for 1 to 2 hours or on low for 3 to 4 hours. Stir in orzo; cover and cook for another 30 to 45 minutes on high.
- Uncover and use a fork to pull chicken out of the slow cooker. Stir contents of slow cooker, then return chicken to slow cooker on top of the orzo mixture.
- Sprinkle Parmesan cheese over chicken. Cover and cook until cheese is melted, about 5 to 10 minutes. Serve with fresh herbs and cracked black pepper if desired.

"The first time I made this, I accidentally used way too many mushrooms and onions, and they took up a ton of space in my slow cooker! Oh well. I got my veggies!"

Veggie Omelet

Recipe Adapted From: primaverakitchen.com

Slow Cooker Size: 4 to 7 quarts
Serves 4 people

Ingredients

- 6 eggs
- ½ cup almond milk
- Salt and ground black pepper, to taste
- 1 garlic clove, minced
- 1 red bell pepper, thinly sliced
- 1 small white onion, finely chopped
- 1 cup spinach, shredded
- 1 cup mozzarella cheese, shredded
- Cherry tomatoes and fresh parsley (optional, for garnish)

Steps

- Coat the inside (including the sides) of the slow cooker with PAM. Set aside.
- In a large mixing bowl, combine eggs, milk, salt, pepper and garlic and whisk well.
- Pour the egg mixture into the slow cooker.
- Add bell peppers, spinach and onions and to the slow cooker.
- Cover and cook on high for 2.5 hours.
- Sprinkle with cheese on top of the omelet and cover.
- Cook until cheese is melted.
- Before serving, garnish with fresh parsley and cherry tomatoes if you wish.

Aired on Facebook LIVE:
4/30/2017

I think I'm causing CEOs a problem because CEOs were led to believe you can't do this.

     #SlowCookerSunday: Leadership, Life and Slow Cooking with CEO and Chef, John Legere

Rainbow Risotto with Peppers

Recipe Adapted From: superhealthykids.com

"I love this recipe. I make it every year in June for Pride Month, on the weekend of Seattle and NYC Pride."

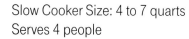

Slow Cooker Size: 4 to 7 quarts
Serves 4 people

Ingredients

- 1 cup long-grain rice
- 1 medium red bell pepper
- 1 medium orange bell pepper
- 1 medium yellow bell pepper
- 1 medium green bell pepper
- ½ cup red cabbage, chopped
- 1¾ cup low-sodium chicken broth

ADD:

- ½ cup milk
- 2 tablespoons butter, unsalted
- 1½ cup, shredded, low-fat Monterey cheese

Steps

- Finely chop all the bell peppers and purple cabbage.
- Combine the rice with the vegetables in the slow cooker and pour chicken broth over it. Set it on high for 2½ hours or on low for about 4 hours. Make sure the rice has absorbed all the liquid.
- Unplug the slow cooker and add milk, butter and Monterey cheese.
- Stir to combine and let sit for 5 minutes. Season with salt.

Aired on Facebook LIVE:
6/26/2016

Baked Apples

Recipe Adapted From: houseofhawthornes.com

Slow Cooker Size: 4 to 7 quarts
Serves 6 people

Ingredients

- 6 large apples
- ¾ cup brown sugar
- 1 teaspoon cinnamon
- 2 tablespoons margarine or butter
- ½ cup apple juice
- ¼ cup walnuts or ¼ cup old-fashioned oats

Steps

- Wash and core apples. You can use a melon baller or paring knife to core the apples. Pare off a 1-inch strip of the skin around the top of the apple to prevent the apples from splitting.
- Mix the brown sugar, cinnamon, margarine and walnuts (or oats) together in a large bowl and fill each apple with the mixture.
- Place apples in the slow cooker and add the apple juice around the bottom of the apples.
- Turn slow cooker on high heat and cook for 2½ to 3 hours until apples are soft when poked with a fork.
- Serve with ice cream and caramel sauce or go old school and just serve as is!

Aired on Facebook LIVE:
10/30/2016

Chicken Cacciatore

Recipe Adapted From: skinnytaste.com

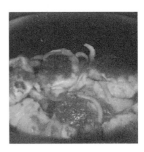

Aired on Facebook LIVE: 5/8/2016

Slow Cooker Size: 4 to 7 quarts
Serves 8 people

Ingredients

- 8 chicken thighs, bone and skin removed
- 1 (28-ounce) can crushed tomatoes
- ½ red bell pepper, sliced into strips
- ½ green bell pepper, sliced into strips
- ½ large onion, sliced
- 1 teaspoon dried oregano
- 1 bay leaf
- Salt and fresh pepper, to taste
- ¼ cup fresh herbs, such as basil or parsley for topping
- 1 to 2 tablespoons of honey (optional)

Steps

Quick method:

- Season chicken with salt and black pepper and place in the slow cooker.
- Pour tomatoes over the chicken, top with onions and peppers, add oregano, bay leaf, honey, salt and pepper, give it a quick stir and cover.
- Set slow cooker on low for 8 hours or on high for 4 hours.
- When the timer beeps, remove the lid and keep the slow cooker on high for 1 hour to help it thicken.

Better method but requires more prep:

- Heat a large skillet over medium-high heat, lightly spray with PAM and brown chicken on both sides for a few minutes, season with salt and pepper. Add to the slow cooker.
- To the skillet, spray with a little more PAM and add onions and peppers. Sauté until juices release and the vegetables become golden; this should take a few minutes. Add to the slow cooker. Pour tomatoes over the chicken and vegetables, add oregano, bay leaf, honey, salt and pepper, give it a quick stir and cover.
- Set slow cooker on low 8 hours or on high 4 hours. Remove bay leaf, adjust salt and pepper and enjoy!

"I added my own twist to this recipe—a little honey! I'm not a big sugar guy, but something about honey just makes this dish sing."

Slow-Roasted Chicken With Vegetables

Recipe Adapted From: tasteofhome.com

Slow Cooker Size: 6 to 7 quarts
Serves 6 people

Ingredients

- 2 medium carrots, peeled, halved lengthwise and cut into 3-inch pieces
- 2 celery ribs, halved lengthwise and cut into 3-inch pieces
- 8 small red potatoes, quartered
- ¾ teaspoon salt, divided
- ⅛ teaspoon pepper
- 1 medium lemon, halved
- 2 garlic cloves, minced
- 1 broiler/fryer chicken (3 to 4 pounds)
- 1 tablespoon dried rosemary, crushed
- 1 tablespoon lemon juice
- 1 tablespoon olive oil
- 2½ teaspoons paprika
- Cooking twine

Steps

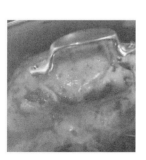

- Place carrots, celery and potatoes in the slow cooker; sprinkle with ¼ teaspoon of salt and pepper. Place lemon halves and garlic in the chicken cavity. Tuck wings under chicken; tie drumsticks together. Place chicken over vegetables in the slow cooker, breast-side up. Mix together rosemary, lemon juice, oil, paprika and remaining salt in a small bowl; rub over chicken.

- Cook, covered, on low until a thermometer inserted in thigh reads at least 170°F and vegetables are tender, about 6 to 8 hours.

- Remove the chicken from the slow cooker; tent with foil. Let stand for 15 minutes before carving. Serve with vegetables.

Aired on Facebook LIVE:
2/12/2017

Apple Pudding Cake

Recipe Adapted From: bunnyswarmoven.net

Slow Cooker Size: 4 to 5 quarts
Serves 10 people

Ingredients

- 2 cups all-purpose flour
- ⅔ cup plus ¼ cup sugar, divided
- 3 teaspoons baking powder
- 1 teaspoon salt
- ½ cup butter, cold
- 1 cup milk
- 4 apples, peeled and diced
- 1½ cups orange juice
- ½ cup honey or light brown sugar
- 2 tablespoons butter, melted
- 1 teaspoon cinnamon

Steps

- Combine the flour, ⅔ cup of sugar, baking powder and salt in a large bowl. Cut the butter into the mixture until you have coarse crumbs.
- Stir the milk into the crumbs just until moistened.
- Grease the bottom and sides of the slow cooker. Spoon the batter into the bottom of the slow cooker and spread out evenly. Place the diced apples evenly over the batter.
- In a bowl, whisk together the orange juice, honey, melted butter, remaining sugar and cinnamon. Pour over the apples.
- Place a clean kitchen towel over the opening of the slow cooker and place the lid on. This keeps condensation from the lid from going into the slow cooker. Cook for 2 to 3 hours on high until apples are tender.
- Serve warm.

"I'm not a big 'sweets' guy, but this recipe is a winner. And bonus—your kitchen's gonna smell incredible!"

Sticky Chicken Wings

Recipe Adapted From: damndelicious.net

Slow Cooker Size: 4 to 7 quarts
Serves 2–3 people

Ingredients

For the chicken:

- 3 pounds chicken wings
- 2 tablespoons cornstarch
- 1 tablespoon sesame seeds
- 2 tablespoons chopped, fresh cilantro leaves

For the sauce:

- ⅓ cup reduced-sodium soy sauce
- ⅓ cup balsamic vinegar
- ⅓ cup brown sugar, packed
- ¼ cup honey
- 3 cloves garlic, minced
- 1 teaspoon hot sauce, or more, to taste
- 1 teaspoon ginger powder
- 1 teaspoon ground pepper
- ½ teaspoon onion powder

Steps

- In a large bowl, whisk together soy sauce, balsamic vinegar, brown sugar, honey, garlic, Sriracha, ginger powder, pepper and onion powder.
- Place wings into the slow cooker. Stir in soy sauce mixture and gently toss to combine.
- Cover and cook on low heat for 3 to 4 hours or on high heat for 1 to 2 hours.
- In a small bowl, whisk together cornstarch and 2 tablespoons of water. Stir in mixture into the slow cooker. Cover and cook on high heat for an additional 10 to 15 minutes or until the sauce has thickened.
- Preheat oven to broil. Line a baking sheet with foil.
- Place wings onto the prepared baking sheet and broil for 2 to 3 minutes or until caramelized and slightly charred.
- Serve immediately with remaining sauce, garnished with sesame seeds and cilantro if desired.

Italian Saucy Chicken Thighs

Recipe Adapted From: cdkitchen.com

Aired on Facebook LIVE: 11/12/2017

Slow Cooker Size: 4 to 7 quarts
Serves 4 people

Ingredients

- 3 pounds bone-in, skinless chicken thighs
- 1 onion, chopped
- 2 cloves garlic, minced
- 1 teaspoon Italian seasoning
- Salt and pepper, to taste
- 1 (15-ounce) can Italia- style tomatoes, diced and undrained
- 1 (8-ounce) can tomato sauce

Steps

- Place the chicken thighs in the bottom of the slow cooker. Top with the chopped onion and minced garlic.
- Sprinkle with the Italian seasoning and add salt and pepper as desired.
- Pour the diced tomatoes and tomato sauce over all. Cover the slow cooker and cook on high for 1 hour, then reduce the heat to low and cook for 5 to 6 more hours or until the chicken is cooked through.

Cheesy Spinach and Mozzarella Rigatoni

Recipe Adapted From: amindfullmom.com

Slow Cooker Size: 4 to 7 quarts
Serves 8 people

Aired on Facebook LIVE: 11/13/2016

Ingredients

- 1 (28-ounce) can tomato puree
- 1 (6-ounce) can tomato paste
- 3 cups water, divided
- 1 tablespoon honey
- 1 tablespoon olive oil
- 2 teaspoons dried oregano
- 1 teaspoon salt
- ½ teaspoon pepper
- ½ teaspoon red pepper flakes (optional)
- 1 (16-ounce) package rigatoni
- 1 (10-ounce) package thawed frozen spinach, squeezed of excess liquid
- 1 cup cottage cheese
- 1 cup mozzarella cheese, shredded
- Fresh parmesan for serving

Steps

- Mix tomato puree, tomato paste, 2 cups water, oil, honey and spices together in the slow cooker. Set to low and cook for 4 to 5 hours.
- Turn slow cooker to high and mix in 1 cup of water, pasta, spinach and cottage cheese. Top with mozzarella cheese. Cover and let cook for about 45 minutes for whole grain pasta and 25 minutes for white pasta.
- Serve with Parmesan cheese.

Chicken Tacos

Recipe Adapted From: buzzfeed.com

Aired on Facebook LIVE: 10/17/2017

Slow Cooker Size: 4 to 7 quarts
Serves 12 people

Ingredients

Taco seasoning:

- 2 teaspoons cumin
- 2 teaspoons oregano
- 1½ teaspoons paprika
- 1 teaspoon chili powder
- ½ teaspoon black pepper
- Salt, to taste

Tacos:

- 1 onion, thinly sliced
- 1 cup corn
- 1 can diced tomatoes, drained
- 1 large jalapeño pepper, deseeded and diced
- 4 cloves garlic, minced
- 1 lime, juiced (2 tablespoons)
- 6 boneless, skinless chicken thighs
- Corn tortillas
- Guacamole
- Salsa

Steps

- In a small bowl, combine the cumin, oregano, paprika, chili powder, pepper and salt and stir to combine. Set aside.
- Place the onion, corn, tomatoes, jalapeño, garlic and lime juice in the slow cooker.
- Place the chicken thighs on top of the veggies and season with half of the taco seasoning. Turn the chicken over and season with the remaining taco seasoning before mixing the chicken and veggies together so that everything is well combined.
- Cook on the high setting for 3 hours or on the low setting for 6 hours until the chicken is cooked through.
- Remove the chicken and slice into small diced pieces, then place them back in the slow cooker. Give the chicken and veggies a good mix and replace the lid.
- Cook the chicken mixture for another 10 minutes so the flavors can marry.
- Using tongs or a slotted spoon, place the chicken taco mixture on corn tortillas and top with your choice of toppings.

Giant Chocolate Chip Cookie

Recipe Adapted From: delish.com

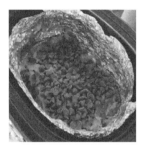   

Aired on Facebook LIVE: 12/4/2016

Slow Cooker Size: 4 to 7 quarts
Serves 8–10 people

Ingredients

- ½ cup (1 stick) butter, softened to room temperature
- ½ cup sugar
- ⅓ cup brown sugar
- 1 large egg
- 1 teaspoon pure vanilla extract
- 1½ cup all-purpose flour
- 1 teaspoon baking soda
- Large pinch salt
- 1½ cup chocolate chips

Steps

- Using two 4- to 5-inch strips of parchment paper, line the bowl of your slow cooker in an X formation. Using an electric mixer, beat butter and sugars until light and fluffy, about 2 minutes. Slowly beat in egg and vanilla extract.

- Add flour, baking soda and salt and stir until fully combined. Fold in chocolate chips. Pour cookie dough into slow cooker and smooth the top with a spatula.

- Cover and cook on high for 2½ to 3 hours (or on low for 5 to 6 hours) or until the cookie is almost completely cooked through and only slightly soft in the center. The cookie can be kept warm in the slow cooker for up to 3 hours. Remove insert from the slow cooker base and place on a cooling rack to cool. Use the parchment paper to remove the cookie; slice and serve.

Index

Lentils

Lentil and Quinoa Chili	94
Red Lentil Curry	60
Vegetarian Lentil Sloppy Joes	38
Vegetarian Lentil Tortilla Soup	90

Pasta

Cheesy Spinach and Mozzarella Rigatoni	144
Chicken Tortellini Soup	100
Parmesan-Herb Chicken and Orzo	124
Spicy Beef Tortellini Soup	64
Stuffed Shells with Spinach	122

Pork

Beer Brats	28
Christmas Ham	44
Jambalaya	76
Scalloped Potatoes and Ham	36

Potatoes

Chicken Curry	79
Corned Beef and Cabbage	20
Filipino Beef Afritada	18
Maine Corn Chowder	104
Melt-In-Your-Mouth Pot Roast	30
Pollo Guisado	54
Pumpkin Chicken Corn Chowder	88
Root Vegetable Stew	95
Scalloped Potatoes and Ham	36
Slow-Roasted Chicken with Vegetables	136

Poultry (see chicken)

Rice

Chipotle-Lime Chicken Thighs with Jamaican Rice	58
Creamy Chicken and Wild Rice Soup	98
Ginger Chicken Congee	78
Rainbow Risotto with Peppers	130

Shrimp

Jambalaya	76

Soups

Chicken Tortellini Soup	100
Chili with Black Beans and Corn	102
Creamy Chicken and Wild Rice Soup	98
Lentil and Quinoa Chili	94
Maine Corn Chowder	104
Spicy Beef Tortellini Soup	64
Split Pea Soup	92
Thai Chicken Soup	108
Turkey Chili	110
Vegetarian Lentil Tortilla Soup	90

Stews

Root Vegetable Stew	95
Tomato Basil Chicken Stew	111

Vegan & Vegetarian

Apple Dump Cake	40
Apple Pudding Cake	140
Baked Apples	132
Cheesy Spinach and Mozzarella Rigatoni	144
Chili with Black Beans and Corn	102
Eggplant Lasagna	120
Giant Chocolate Chip Cookie	148
Lentil and Quinoa Chili	94
Maine Corn Chowder	104
Polenta	43
Red Lentil Curry	60
Rainbow Risotto with Peppers	130
Root Vegetable Stew	95
Split Pea Soup	92
Stuffed Shells with Spinach	122
Veggie Omelet	126
Vegetarian Lentil Sloppy Joes	38
Vegetarian Lentil Tortilla Soup	90

...AND
HAPPY
SLOW
COOKER
SUNDAY!